PERIOD.

REVISED and UPDATED
with A Parents' Guide

JoAnn Gardner-Loulan
Bonnie Lopez
Marcia Quackenbush

Illustrated by Marcia Quackenbush

VOLCANO
· PRESS ·

Library of Congress Cataloging in Publication Data:

    Loulan, JoAnn Gardner—
       Period / JoAnn Gardner-Loulan, Bonnie Lopez, Marcia Quackenbush;
    illustrated by Marcia Quackenbush.—Updated with a parent and
    teacher's guide.
        p. cm.
       Summary: Discusses the physical and psychological changes at the
    onset of menstruation. Includes a guide for parents and teachers.
      ISBN 0-912078-88-X
      1. Menstruation—Juvenile literature.   [1. Menstruation.]
    I. Lopez, Bonnie. II. Quackenbush, Marcia. III. Title.
    QP263.L68   1990
    612.6'62—dc20

                                      90-46065
                                        CIP
                                        AC

Order directly from:
Volcano Press, Inc.
P.O. Box 270
Volcano CA 95689 USA
Phone: (209) 296-3445   FAX (209) 296-4515

Send $9.95 for each book; include $3.00 shipping & handling for the first book ordered, $.75 for each additional book. California residents please add 6% sales tax.

Schools, Agencies, Organizations: Please contact us directly for quantity discount rates.

Printed in the United States of America

Production by David Charlsen & Others

Contents

This book is dedicated to Billie Gardner Loulan, R.N.

We appreciate those women who allowed us to print their experiences on these pages. There were many other friends who helped and supported us throughout the writing of this book. We would especially like to thank:

Joani Blank, Publisher
Sandy Fujita, Author
Jeanne McFarland, R.N.
Katharine and Larry Moore of Ramparts Press
Nici Muller, M.D.
New Seed Press
JoAnn Ogden, Printer
Our Health Clinic
Judith Supnik, Printer/Editor

Layout and design by Kathleen Moore
                              Marcia Quackenbush

Introduction

Three of us, Bonnie, JoAnn and Marcia, wrote this book for girls who are growing up. We thought it would be important to have a book explaining some of the changes all girls go through. We talked about all kinds of things as we wrote the book, and we learned from the experiences that we shared with our friends. We've put some of the things they said in this book.

It might be interesting for you to talk to your friends as you're going through the chapters. We all have a lot to learn from each other.

Have a good time reading and looking at the pictures.

So Many Changes

Magazines, billboards, television and movies
show girls and women who are tall and slim,
have faces with no pimples, never wear glasses
and seem to have no big problems at all. Not
too many people really are that way, but when
we see so many women like that it can make us
feel that somehow our body or face or hair is
just not right.

I used to drive myself crazy when I was growing up because I had no waist. Everyone I saw at school or on the street had tiny waists — everyone but me. So I would diet and not let myself eat things that everyone else ate. Know what happened? I lost weight and still had no waist! Then I finally caught on that I had a certain body type and no matter what I ate, I would just go from my rib cage to my hips in a straight line. I am feeling much better about myself just knowing everyone has a different body.

2

I used to hate the hair on my upper lip. My hair is black, so it's really noticeable. Then I met a girl at school who was just like me and I would watch her when the kids teased her. It really surprised me because it didn't bother her at all! That's when I stopped worrying.

We live in a crazy, mixed-up world because many girls and women think that everyone else has the longest hair or smallest feet, nicest smile or prettiest eyes. But what most people have in common is that we have bodies that can do so many different things, no matter what color, size or shape we are.

3

We can walk or read or sing or take bubble baths; we can taste wonderful foods or throw balls or listen to birds chirping or dance or run or think or laugh. Sometimes bodies can make us feel soooo gooood! Can you imagine what you'd do without one?

Some of us have bodies that are disabled. This means that some part of the body can't be moved (is paralyzed) or moves uncontrollably (is spastic). Maybe we are blind or deaf, or we have one leg or arm that didn't grow as long as the other. Or a part of our body had to be removed (amputated) because something was wrong with it. Lots of people have these kinds of bodies and it's important that we all learn to appreciate the wonderful things our bodies can do for us. Disabled people can do things that "able-bodied" people can't. "Able-bodied" people can do things disabled people can't. This doesn't mean one person is better than another, it just means that we're different.

One reason we all have different bodies is because of our parents. They have passed some things about their bodies on to us, like the color of our eyes, skin and hair, or how tall we are. You might have your mother's hair color and your father's eyes. But sometimes we think we really can't be happy unless we look like our favorite movie star or girlfriend or aunt. Being comfortable with your own body is important. Learning to love your own specialness is a big part of growing up.

Since your birth, your body has been changing and growing. When you get to be ten or twelve or fourteen, more obvious changes begin to happen. You may begin getting pimples, and the hair under your arms and on your legs may be easier to see. Some people start to sweat (perspire), and perspiration may smell different as you grow older. Your hips get bigger, your breasts begin to grow, and your body actually begins to change shape. The area around your nipple, called the *areola* (ah-REE-oh-la), becomes a little raised and might change color. You might begin growing taller at this age. You will also probably start growing hair on the area below your belly button, close to your legs. This is called *pubic* (PEW-bik) hair.

When I was growing pubic hair, I thought something was wrong with me so I began pulling it out with tweezers. I realized it was normal when I just couldn't pull it out fast enough. But it sure was scary at first!

It seems that all of a sudden you are running around with a new body, and it may take some getting used to. You may be the first one in school to show breasts or the last one to gain some weight and start looking older. Maybe your parents or older sisters and brothers will tease and embarrass you. Boys or other girls may make fun of your new bra. You may not believe this, but few of us are comfortable with these changes.

Can you think of three things you really like about your body? Do you like the color or softness of your skin? How about your legs or hands? You really are a special person, and the more you realize that, the better you will feel about yourself.

So Many Parts

Some of the changes your body goes through as you grow older are easy to see, but others go on inside of your body. Even though you don't usually see these changes, they affect your life and the way you feel.

There are a lot of diagrams in this chapter and the next. These diagrams will help explain things, but remember that every woman is different and none of the diagrams will really be exactly like you or anyone else. They can give you an idea of shapes and where things are.

There are quite a few organs inside of us. One way to look at them is by a "cross section" diagram. This is a cross section of an apple. You see the lines and shapes and seeds of the inside of the apple.

The internal organs we will be talking about in this chapter are organs only girls and women have.

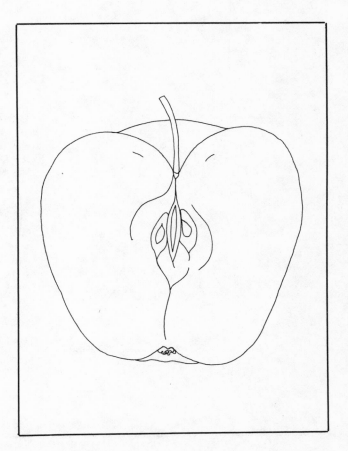

The body of a girl is different from that of a woman, but it's hard to say exactly when a girl becomes a woman. From the time we are born, bodies start the kinds of changes this book is all about. In a young girl, internal organs (organs that are inside of us) look something like this:

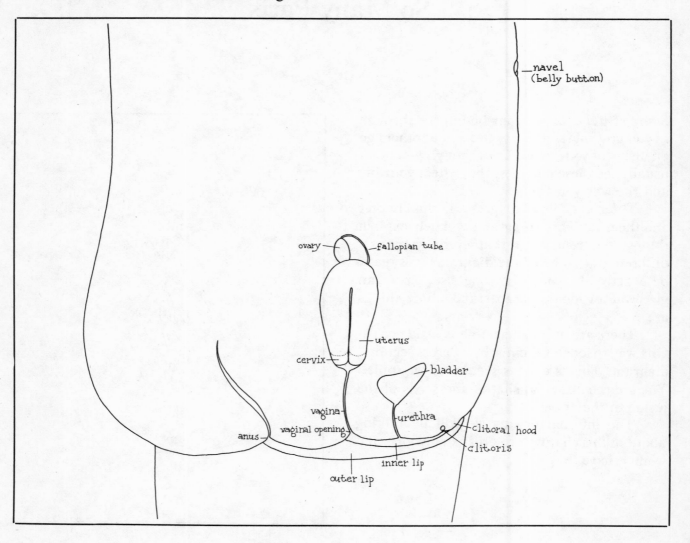

navel
(belly button)

ovary — fallopian tube

uterus

cervix

bladder

vagina

urethra

anus

vaginal opening

clitoral hood

clitoris

inner lip

outer lip

This diagram is of an adult woman:

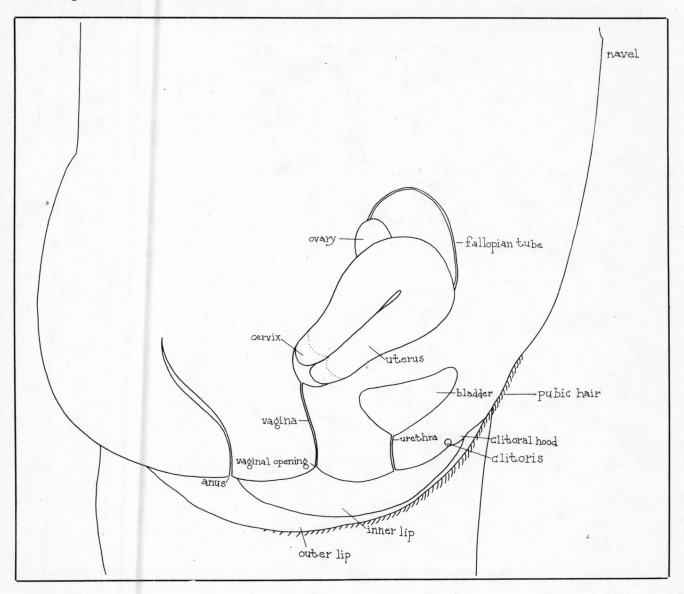

navel

ovary — — fallopian tube

cervix

uterus

bladder — pubic hair

vagina —

urethra

clitoral hood

clitoris

vaginal opening

anus

inner lip

outer lip

On these two pages are diagrams which also
show the differences between girls and women.

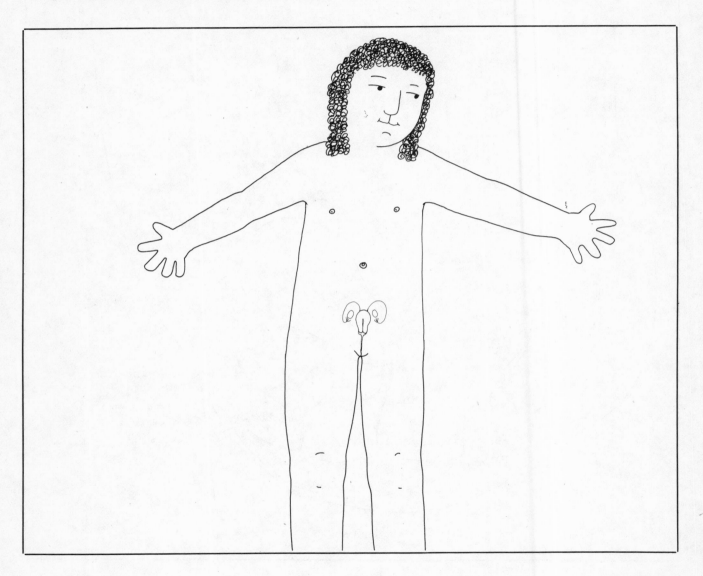

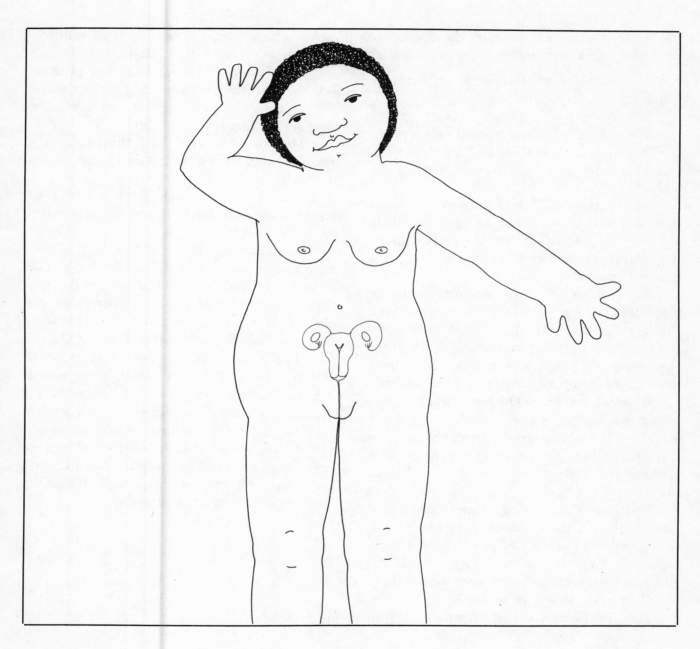

15

Here is a list of some of these organs, what they are called and why we have them:

The *anus* (AY-nus) is the opening through which bowel movements pass.

The *uterus* (YOU-ter-us) is where an egg grows into a baby when a woman is pregnant.

The *vagina* (va-JAI-nah) is a passageway that leads from the uterus to the outside of the body.

The *cervix* (SER-vix) protects delicate tissues in the uterus. It has an opening which leads from the uterus to the vagina. The opening of the cervix is only as big around as a piece of spaghetti.

The *ovaries* (OH-vah-reez) are the organs that hold all the *ova* (OH-vah) (the eggs). One egg is called an *ovum* (OH-vum). The cross section shows only one ovary, but in the front view diagram, you can see both. They hold many more eggs than are ever needed or used. There are about 400,000 eggs in each ovary. When a baby girl is born, all those eggs are already in her little ovaries. Ovaries are sort of spongy and the eggs are tucked away in little pockets and folds. One egg is only as big as the tip of a needle.

Every so often, an egg travels from one ovary to the uterus. It moves along one of the *fallopian tubes* (fa-LOH-pee-an). (This is explained more in the next chapter.) Each fallopian tube is about four inches long and no bigger around than a piece of thread. These tubes are lined with very tiny little hairs. If you looked at the inside of one through a microscope, it would look like soft velvet.

The *hymen* (HI-men) is a thin piece of skin that surrounds the opening to the vagina.

The *vaginal opening* (VA-jin-al) is the opening leading into the vagina.

The *urethra* (you-REE-thrah) is the opening where *urine* (YUR-rin) passes from the body.

The *bladder* (BLAD-der) is where your body holds your urine until you go to the bathroom.

The *inner lips* are folds of skin that surround the urethra and vaginal opening. The *outer lips* are pads of skin that protect the very delicate tissues in this area. When you get older, hair grows on your outer lips. This adds protection and is called *pubic* (PEW-bik) hair.

The *clitoris* (CLIT-tor-iss) is a small bump of skin. It's very sensitive because it contains many nerve endings. Because the clitoris is so sensitive, there is a cover to protect it. This cover is called the *clitoral hood*.

Genitals (JEN-a-tulls) refers to the entire area we've been talking about. The inner and outer lips, clitoris, urethra, vaginal opening and anus make up the genitals.

The uterus is an interesting organ. It seems like it should be very large since a baby might have to fit inside of it someday. But it really isn't big at all. It's about the size of your fist. When a woman becomes pregnant, the uterus grows in size with the baby, and after the baby is born, the uterus becomes small again. There are some cut-outs on page 89. One shows the size of the uterus of a woman about twenty-five years old. The other shows the size of a twelve-year-old girl's uterus. If you cut out these pictures and hold them up to your stomach, under your belly button, you might get a better idea of how big your uterus is.

The vagina is another organ which seems like it should be larger because a baby has to travel through the vagina when it's being born. But during birth, the vagina stretches. The sides of the vagina, called the vaginal walls, usually lie close together, touching, like a balloon with no air in it. There isn't a large space at all.

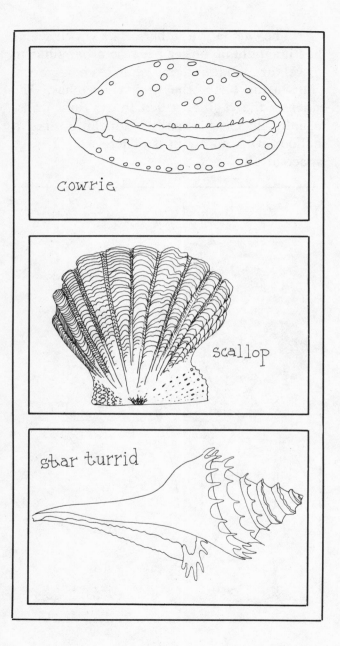

cowrie

scallop

star turrid

In Chapter 1 we talked about the changes that you see and feel as you grow older, like getting taller or having your breasts grow. This chapter described some of the changes that go on inside of you, changes you can't see. Even though our genitals are outside of our bodies, we don't see them very often.

Like most parts of our bodies, genitals change as we get older too, but often we don't notice. We rarely look at our genitals because they are tucked away. When you're young, it looks as if you don't have any inner lips at all. They're very small. When you're older, your inner lips grow larger, but exactly how much they grow is different for all of us.

Just like her smile or the color of her hair, everyone's genitals are a little different. It might help to think of flowers or sea shells — no two flowers will ever be quite the same even if they're the same kind of flower.

arabis

iris

hyacinth

marguerite

tiger lily

phlox

Menstruation

One of the things that happens when a girl grows up is that she will begin to menstruate (MEN-stroo-ate). What exactly is this mysterious thing called *menstruation* (MEN-stroo-AY-shun)? Let's talk about it.

At a certain time in your life, maybe when you're ten, or fourteen, or eighteen, the *hormones* (HOR-mones) in your body become very active. Hormones are chemicals your body makes. These hormones, in their own special way, begin telling your body to be alert, pay attention, and start doing things it's never done before. There are hundreds and hundreds of these messages. In this chapter, only a few will be mentioned. It would be confusing to try to keep track of all of them.

One of the first things to happen is that an egg works its way out of one of your ovaries. (Remember that this egg will be no larger than the point of a needle.) This tiny egg floating around wants to get from the ovary to the uterus. That seems like a difficult thing to do, especially since the egg doesn't have any wings to fly with or wheels to roll with. But each fallopian tube has these teeny tiny little hairs at the end of it, almost like fingers. They swoosh back and forth like waves in the ocean, trying to help the egg inside the tube. When this happens, the egg travels all the way through the fallopian tube to the uterus.

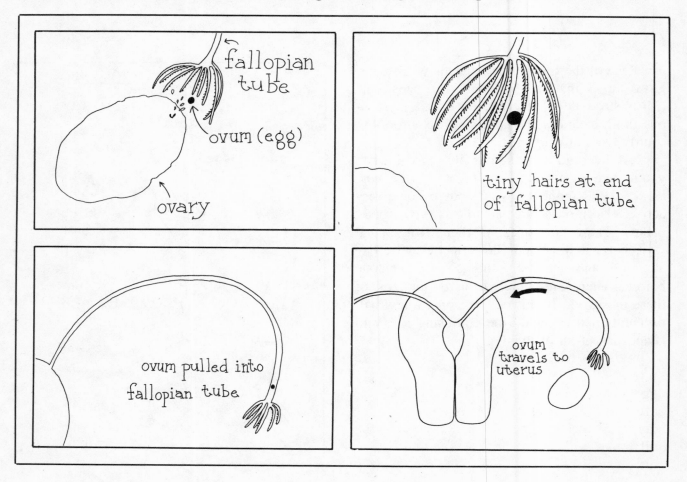

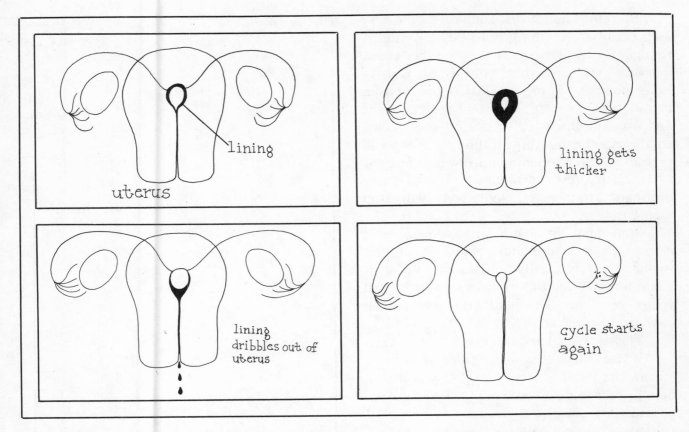

lining

uterus

lining gets thicker

lining dribbles out of uterus

cycle starts again

At the same time this happens, your uterus begins building up a lining of healthy, fresh tissue and blood. (You can picture what a "lining" is if you think of wallpaper that lies on the walls inside of a house.) By the time the egg reaches the uterus, the lining of the uterus is full and rich and soft. If the egg is going to stay for awhile and become a baby, this lining will make its stay healthy and comfortable. But most of the time, the egg just visits and then passes on through. If the egg isn't staying in the uterus, the uterus doesn't need all that lining, so the lining, made up of blood and tiny pieces of tissue dribbles out. It passes through the small opening in the cervix, down through the vagina and out the vaginal opening. About two weeks later, another egg pops out of one of the ovaries, and the whole cycle starts again. This is what menstruation is all about.

It seems like all this shouldn't take very long because everything is so busy. Actually, though, the whole menstrual cycle takes about a month. The part where your uterus is dribbling blood and lining may last anywhere from two to eight days. It's different for every girl and woman. Once you've started your menstrual cycle, the monthly dribbling of blood will probably keep happening until you're forty or fifty. Then those hormones will send more messages around and your body will stop menstruating.

Something else that happens to many girls is that another kind of fluid comes out of their vagina. There is usually not very much of it. It might be clear and thin. It might be sticky and yellow or white. The fluid may have a faint odor, or no smell at all.

This is normal and healthy.

If the fluid is a dark color (brown or green), the smell is very strong, or you itch or burn in your vagina, you should talk to a grown-up and see a doctor.

The next few chapters talk about what menstruation may feel like for you, what you do to catch your menstrual blood, and how to keep an eye on your cycle and stay healthy.

Pads, Pins or Tampons?

Seventy-five years ago, girls and women placed folded pieces of cloth inside their underpants to catch their menstrual blood. Today we have so many menstrual products to choose from, it's almost hard to decide which is best to use. It will be easier to choose a product when you know what each is like and how it is used.

SANITARY PADS or SANITARY NAPKINS

Sanitary pads come in different sizes and are made of material like soft cotton. Some pads are used with a special belt which holds them in place.

A Sanitary belt looks like this:

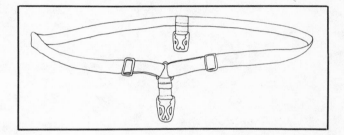

A pad is fastened to the belt like this:

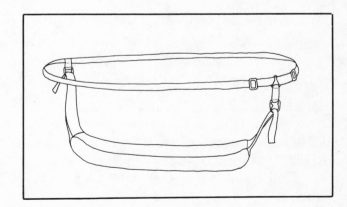

There are also pads made to be worn without belts or pins. They have a sticky strip that helps them stay in place on your underpants and come off easily when you change pads.

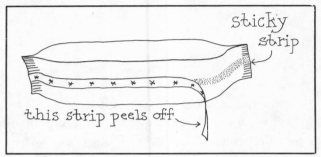

sticky strip

this strip peels off

With pads, one side faces toward your body and one toward your underpants. The side that faces your pants usually has a strip, colored string or some design on it, and the side that faces you is usually plain.

cross-section of a sanitary pad:

soft cotton pad

plastic shield to keep blood from staining clothes

It fits under your clothes. If you don't have a belt or don't want to use one, you can also use safety pins and pin a pad onto your underpants.

The first time I wore a pad, it felt so huge and bulky. I was sure everyone could tell I was on my period. I was surprised when I finally looked into a mirror and saw that the pad didn't show at all.

It's true that for most girls, a pad feels funny at first. But pads fit close to your body and really don't show. If a large pad isn't comfortable, try a smaller size.

TAMPONS

Tampons are another product used to catch menstrual blood. They are made of soft material pressed together into this kind of shape:

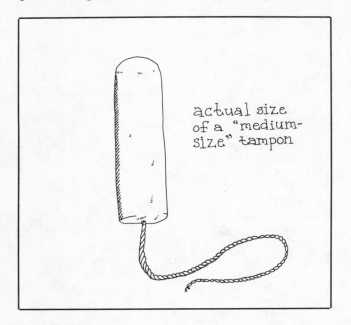

actual size of a "medium-size" tampon

There is a string at the end of the tampon. Tampons fit inside the vagina and the string hangs down through the vaginal opening. When you want to remove a tampon, you pull gently on the string and it comes right out.

Tampons, like pads, come in different sizes. There are junior (small), regular (medium), super (large) and extra large sizes. The first time you try a tampon, a smaller size will probably be easiest.

Some tampons come with an applicator which helps guide the tampon into the vagina. It's thrown away when the tampon's in place. There are cardboard, plastic and stick applicators. Some tampons don't have any applicator. You just use your finger to guide the tampon into your vagina.

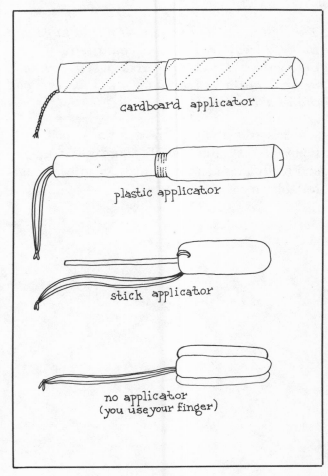

cardboard applicator

plastic applicator

stick applicator

no applicator
(you use your finger)

If a tampon is put in the right way, you probably won't be able to feel it at all, but the first time may be confusing.

There are directions included in every box of tampons. Be sure you read them carefully if you're not sure how to use tampons. You can talk with your mother or with a friend who has used tampons before, and this can help too.

If you do use tampons, it is important to change them at least four times a day (every four to six hours). You might want to use tampons during the day and a pad while you sleep at night. This helps your vagina stay clean and fresh.

There is a rare disease called "Toxic Shock Syndrome." Not very many people have ever gotten this disease. But most women and girls who have had Toxic Shock Syndrome got it because they did not change their tampons often enough. To make sure you stay healthy, change your tampons every four to six hours.

Girls and women using menstrual pads during their periods instead of tampons do not need to worry about this disease, but they will still want to change their pads every few hours.

Some girls are afraid they might lose a tampon in their vagina. A tampon really can't get lost inside of you — there's nowhere for it to go. The opening to the uterus is too small for a tampon to get through and the muscles of the vagina keep it from falling out.

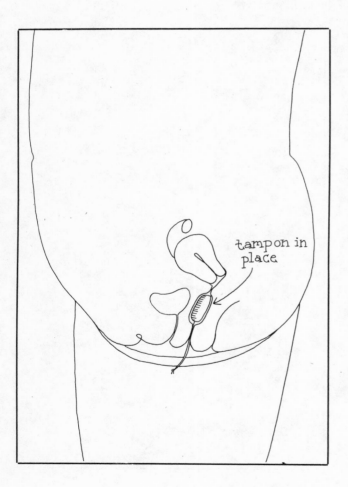

tampon in place

Most girls use pads when they first begin their periods. Later you might want to try tampons. The most important thing is for you to be comfortable with your choice. Each girl will find the product that suits her best.

Pads should be changed at least twice a day, more often when menstrual flow is heavy. Tampons should be changed at least four times a day. When you've finished with a pad or tampon, wrap it up in toilet paper, tissues or newspaper and throw it away. Some people flush tampons down the toilet, but this can clog up some toilets and cause quite a problem.

Once I started my period very late Sunday night and I didn't have any pads or tampons. I got a clean washcloth and folded it so it would comfortably fit me, and used it like a pad. I just rinsed it out in cold water the next morning. It worked very well.

If you are ever caught on your period without pads or tampons, remember what our grandmothers did before the days of menstrual products. Some women even today prefer using a washcloth or similar cloth instead of store bought menstrual pads or tampons.

You may see ads in magazines about vaginal sprays and *douches* (DOOSH-es). A *douche* (DOOSH) is a liquid used to wash the vagina. Vaginal sprays are supposed to help keep you "clean and fresh." But it's been found that, for many women, sprays actually cause infections or rashes. Your vagina cleans itself naturally (like your eyes). The only reason for using a douche is if you have a medical problem and a doctor or health worker suggests you douche.

I Have a Question About That

I had so many questions and scaries about menstruation. No one ever mentioned what was going to happen to me. I saw a film on menstruation in school a year after I began my period. Big help!

Menstruation is a big event in our lives. How we feel about it depends on what our mothers, friends, older sisters, grandmothers or aunts have said. If no one talks about menstruation, it can be very puzzling.

Bodies go through many changes, especially during the teens, and it can help to know what to expect. It's normal to have questions about menstruation. Many girls wonder how old they will be when they begin their periods or how they will know they have started menstruating.

I was upset that I hadn't started menstruating by the time I was sixteen. It seemed like all my girlfriends had already begun having periods. Even my younger sister was menstruating before I was! I was glad when I finally started.

*

When I first menstruated, I bled quite a bit. It scared me because I didn't expect so much blood. Now I know that that's the right amount of blood for my body.

Beginning to menstruate is a unique experience. No one can say exactly what it's going to be like for you, but the more you know about menstruation, the easier it will be.

Menstruation is as normal and natural for girls and women as eating or sleeping. It's a sign that we're changing and it happens at different times for all of us. Some of us begin to menstruate when we're young — maybe nine or ten years old. Some of us don't begin until we're seventeen or eighteen.

Because everyone's body is different, menstruation starts at different times. Most girls probably begin at twelve or thirteen. It's not better to begin menstruating at one age or another. It doesn't mean you're more grown up if you start your periods at age ten, or immature if you start at eighteen. Usually your body knows just the perfect time for *you* to begin menstruating.

I wondered how much blood was going to come out of my vagina. Was it going to gush out?

The amount of blood varies from girl to girl, especially during the first couple years of menstruation. A girl may lose as little as one tablespoon of blood or up to six tablespoons in each cycle. The blood doesn't come out all at once. It dribbles and drips out, and a menstrual period may last from two to eight days. Some girls lose more blood on the first day and less on the following days. Some bleed more on the second day. The way each girl menstruates is different.

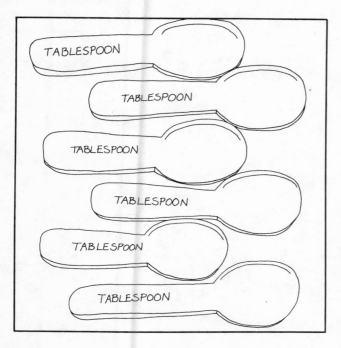

You might want to try on a pad before you ever start your period. This way you can find out how to put one on and what it's like to wear one. It might be uncomfortable or awkward at first, but planning ahead may clear up confusions now rather than on the first day of your period. Experiment. If you wear a pad that feels very bulky and uncomfortable, try a mini-pad. They're smaller and might be better for you. *You* decide what's best for your body.

What if I start in the middle of my math class?

You also might want to think about what you're going to do if you start your period at school. Here are some suggestions:

The first thing you'll want to do is excuse yourself from class. Let your teacher know it is important that you leave the room. If you carry a purse and happen to have a sanitary pad with you, everything should be fine. You have probably practiced beforehand and will already know how to use it.

If you don't have a pad with you, your school might have a machine in the girl's bathroom that sells them for ten cents. But what if your school doesn't have a machine, or you don't have a dime, or there is a machine and you have a dime but the machine is empty? Usually the nurse's office will have sanitary pads available for situations like this, so try there next.

If blood has gotten on your underpants, you can probably wait until you get home to wash them out. If you are uncomfortable or blood is showing on your clothes, you should be able to get an excuse from the school nurse to go home and change your clothes.

Once you have started menstruating, you will have a better idea of when your period will begin each month. You can be prepared by carrying a sanitary pad with you, but if your period ever surprises you, the few steps just mentioned should help out.

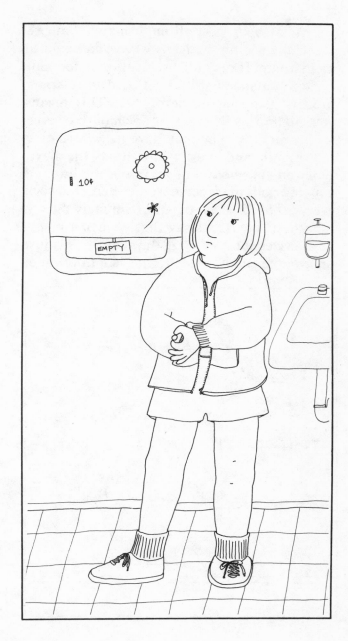

Your body goes through many changes, especially during the teens when you begin to menstruate. It may take several years for your cycle to balance out and get used to this new process going on inside of you. This means you might miss a period for one month or even for six months. You may have heavy bleeding one month and hardly any at all the next. Later on your body will get into a rhythm and your period may come somewhere between every 26 to 32 days, or approximately once a month. Many books say that women's menstrual cycles come every 28 days, but this is just an average and not the "right" length of time.

A good way to keep track of your period is by marking the days you menstruate on a calendar. You will get an idea of how long you menstruate as well as how many days there are between periods. Menstrual cycles are measured from the day one period begins to the day the next period begins. Once you've started menstruating, if it seems that your cycle isn't regular, you may want to tell somebody (your mother or someone else you feel comfortable with), and see a doctor.

Families and friends can react so differently when a girl begins her period. Sometimes it makes us proud, sometimes embarrassed.

When I began menstruating, my mother told my older brothers, my father, and even the neighbors! Even now I feel sort of embarrassed when I menstruate.

My family had a very special dinner the night I began my period. I felt very proud and good about it and felt a lot of love from my family. I was growing up and they knew it.

It might be interesting for you to find out similar experiences your mother or friends had when they began menstruating. Sometimes it's comforting to talk to someone when something new is happening to you and you feel like you're the only one in the whole world who is different.

I enjoy talking about my thoughts and feelings with my friends. I used to be uncomfortable asking my friends certain questions. I got over it because I found people love to talk about themselves. For instance, I would have a strange dream and would think something was wrong with me. The more people I talked to, the more I found out my dreams were not that different from other peoples'.

The same goes for menstruation — the more we talk to people, the more we find out that our experiences, feelings and thoughts can be similar.

43

Girls and women may get cramps when they menstruate. These cramps can hurt. Some have uncomfortable cramps while others hardly feel any difference at all when they menstruate. Cramps happen when your uterus, which is a muscle, contracts, similar to the way the muscles in your arm tighten up (or contract) when you make a fist.

44

If you do get cramps, there are several things you can do that might help.

Warmth causes muscles to relax and can help ease cramps. A hot water bottle or heating pad on your stomach may help. (But remember, hot water bottles and heating pads can cause burns if they're used for too long or they're too hot. Check it out with your mother or someone else before using one to make sure you know how to use it correctly.)

A warm bath or drinking something hot like tea or hot chocolate may make you feel better.

Taking a slow walk may help your cramps go away.

Sometimes just rubbing or massaging your stomach can make you feel better. You might try lying on your back with your knees up; move your knees in a small circle. This is a kind of massage too.

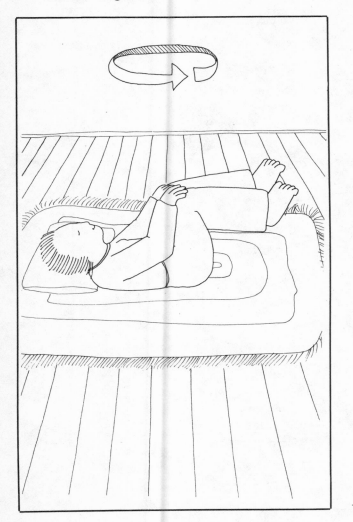

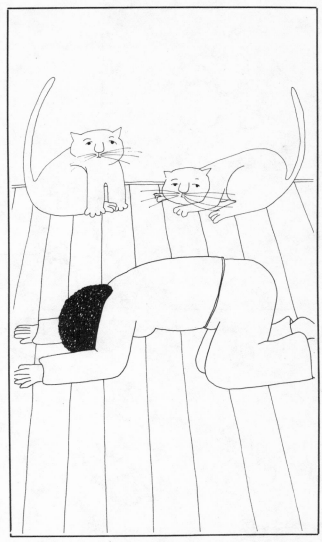

Or just try lying in this position. It feels good because your uterus is hanging down, which helps it relax.

Eating lightly before your period may help. This is because your intestines are packed into your body very close to your uterus. If you've eaten a lot of pizza and hot fudge sundaes, your large intestines get filled up and take more room. Your uterus gets swollen during the first day or two or three of your period, so it takes up more room in the body. By eating lightly, you make more room for your uterus and it is less likely to cramp. Try it out some-time if you are having a lot of cramping.

When you menstruate, you should do what feels right for you. Some of us can do anything we want when we're menstruating. Some of us can't. Since we're all so different, we have to decide what's best for our own bodies. After all, no one knows your body better than *you* do.

When I had bad cramps one day, several of my friends thought I was acting silly because I didn't want to go get some ice cream with them. They made me feel embarrassed only because I was trying to take care of myself. Now that I think about it, I was silly, but only for letting them make me feel embarrassed.

For me, having my period was never any big deal. I've never had bad cramps and menstruation doesn't slow me down a bit. I still run and work and do everything I always do. If anything, I guess I have a little more energy during my period than at other times.

*

I used to hate it when I got my period. I thought it got in the way of wanting to do things, like playing basketball. I loved basketball. But now I think of menstruation as my body telling me that everything inside of me is working and that I'm healthy. For me, it's also a time to sit back, relax and be nice to myself. I might make myself a favorite cup of tea and read a book I haven't had time to read. Or I might just sit there and listen to music or daydream. Now, I almost feel like I'm on vacation.

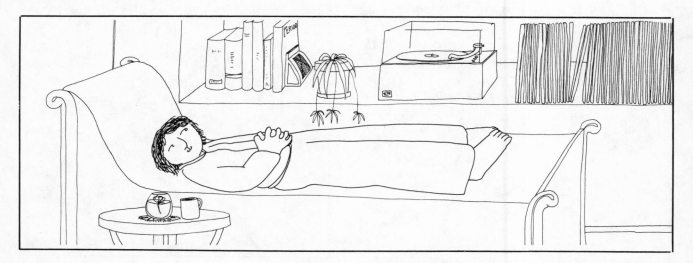

Some people say that it isn't a good idea to go swimming when you are menstruating. Swimming isn't harmful at all. Cool water may make you stop bleeding for awhile and hot water (like a hot bath) may make you bleed a little more heavily. Swimming is okay if you feel like it. You just might be more comfortable wearing a tampon since a pad would get very wet and squishy.

Remember, whatever you do during your period, whether it's playing basketball, reading a book or swimming, really depends on how you feel. There's no right or wrong thing as long as you do what's comfortable for your body.

You may have heard that when you have your period, you have an odor about you that other people can smell. Because heat and air and odors float upwards, we're usually the only ones who can smell our own menstrual blood (if we smell it at all). As long as you wash your genitals with soap and water as usual (or more often if you want to), and change your pad or tampon when necessary, you probably won't have any problems with odor. You may think you're smelly and bothering everyone who comes within two feet of you, but that's because you're so aware of yourself — not because you smell.

During your period, you might get some blood on your underpants. This is very common. If blood stains your pants, use cold water to rinse them out first. It works really well. Then plain old soap and water should get them clean. You could use bleach as a last resort, especially with old stains.

I grew up in a small town, so I knew everyone who worked at the drug store. It was awful for me to have to buy menstrual pads from people I knew, so I always asked my mother to buy them for me.

Sometimes having to go into a store and buy pads or tampons is awkward or embarrassing. It feels like everyone is watching, especially the boys. But, like anything we do again and again, it's not such a big deal after awhile.

Lots of different things have been covered in this chapter. A few of your questions may have been answered, but probably some have been missed. When new questions come up, perhaps you'll talk to somebody you're comfortable with about them.

Why Do I Feel This Way?

As we grow older, we are able to see many changes in our bodies and sometimes our feelings and emotions are changing too. It's natural to have new ideas and feelings at different times in our lives, but because you can't see or touch them, emotions can be confusing.

You may find when you start menstruating that your period affects the way you feel. There are different kinds of feelings girls and women may have and, like so many other things, no two people feel exactly the same. We talked to a lot of women and girls who menstruate and asked them how they feel just before, during or after their periods, and here's what some of them said:

Carol: "When I'm having my period, I feel like I'm just one part of this big exciting world. My menstrual cycle makes me feel like part of the world's cycles — seasons, day and night. It's nice."

Cathy: "I know I'm healthy when my periods are healthy."

Mary: "Sometimes just before my period, I feel sad and don't know why."

Linda: "I always feel much better about my plants when I'm on my period. I love to sing to them and I think they listen better."

Roxanne: "I write better poems when I'm menstruating."

Lyn: "Usually, I don't mind spending an evening alone, but around the time I menstruate, I feel very lonely if people aren't always around me."

Jennifer: "I always love to take walks in the woods or along the beach, especially when I'm on my period."

Lisa: "Oh, I always feel so ugly when I menstruate. My face usually breaks out and I don't like that at all."

Amy: "I like to take care of myself a lot when I'm having my period. I dress up or buy a new scarf or something."

Ellen: "It seems like sometimes when I'm about to menstruate, I get an urge to reorganize shelves, closets, books. And I have a really good time doing it."

Janet: "If I get cramps, they just make me feel bad and it's hard to have fun that day."

Yvette: "I can get *so* mad sometimes about such little things. Right around the time I menstruate, my temper is very short."

Inez: "I love to spend time with lots of friends when I'm on my period."

Jackie: ". . . and I like to spend lots of time all by myself."

Gloria: "Sometimes I feel like no one understands any-thing I'm trying to say."

Esther: "If I have time, I always love to bake bread when I'm having my period."

Emily: "I seem to have so little energy the first day of my period."

Delores: "I have more energy than ever about the time I
start my period."

Toni: "Seems like I spend a lot of time thinking about serious things, expecially when I'm menstruating."

Laura: "I get hungry for certain foods a day or two before my period. I'll get a real craving for strawberries or scrambled eggs, and I'll raid the refrigerator late at night."

Erica: "I feel so many things, all the time. The best part of being healthy and having my period is that I feel joyous and alive."

There's no one way you *have* to feel or are supposed to feel when you're menstruating. Your period might not make you feel any different at all. Once again, part of what's so wonderful about us is that we are all so different about many things.

What's A Pelvic Exam?

A *pelvic* (PEL-vick) exam is an exam where a doctor or other medical worker checks female organs inside and outside our bodies. A nurse practitioner, gynecologist or regular doctor can do this exam. A *gynecologist* (GUY-nuh-KOL-oh-jist) is a doctor specially trained to take care of these female parts.

Just like regular visits to the dentist, having a pelvic exam is very important. Next time you see your doctor, let him or her know you have started your period. Ask your doctor when you should begin to have regular pelvic exams.

By the time you are an adult woman, you should have a pelvic exam every year. It is always better for your body to be checked regularly instead of waiting until you're sick. Regular check-ups can prevent sickness, and that's important!

I was twenty when I had my first pelvic exam. Oh, was I embarrassed! I went alone, trying to act real grown up and like I knew what was going on, but I was scared. I didn't ask what was going to happen to me and no one told me. This made it hard to go back a year later for my second pelvic exam.

Your first pelvic exam doesn't have to be a scary experience, especially if you know what is going on before it happens. Just reading this chapter may make your first exam easier for you.

When you first get to the doctor's office or clinic, you will be asked to fill out a medical history. For instance, a doctor will want to know what diseases you or your family has had, the length of your menstrual period and the date of your last period. You also might want to tell the nurse or doctor that this will be your first pelvic exam.

If your mother or a girlfriend can go with you, it might make you feel better too. If you'd like to have her go into the exam room with you, call ahead to make sure it's okay with your doctor. The doctor will probably say it's all right, but if not, and if it's important to you, you might want to find another doctor.

You will be asked to come into an exam room. Make sure you go to the bathroom before your exam. This will make it more comfortable for you. Once in the room, a nurse or health worker will ask you to undress and give you a paper dress to put on.

The doctor will first examine your breasts. This is done by gently pressing all around your breasts. She will be checking for any abnormal lumps or breast tissues that might be signs of disease. She can show you how to do a breast exam yourself. You'll want to learn to do this so you can check your breasts regularly between pelvic exams.

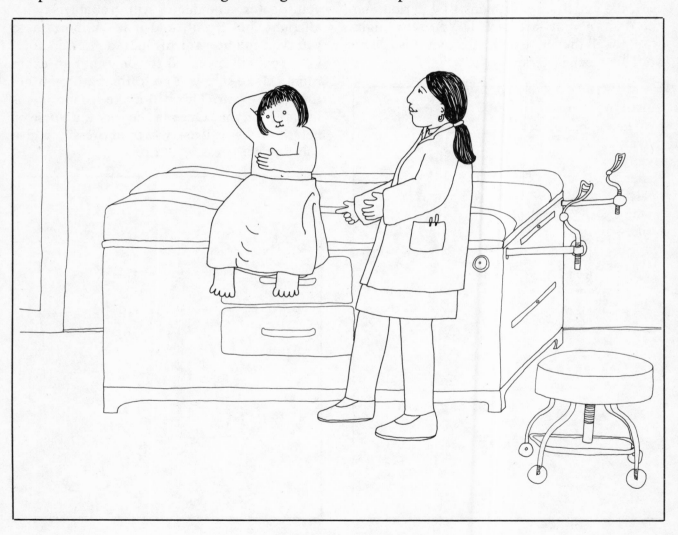

Next, your genitals and internal organs will be checked. You will be asked to lie down and put your feet on something called "stirrups." One kind is made so your feet rest on them. Another kind of stirrups is made so the backs of your knees rest on them. Your knees and legs will be spread open so the genital area is easier to see.

For many girls and women, this is the most embarrassing part of the exam. We're just not used to showing a very delicate and private part of ourselves, especially to strangers. This part of the exam might be easier for you if you go to a woman doctor or health worker. But don't forget, whether it's a woman or a man, your doctor has done this hundreds of times. It may be new to you, but she is used to it and is most concerned with your health.

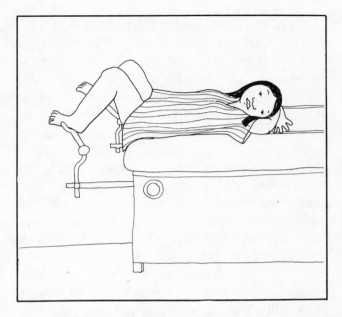

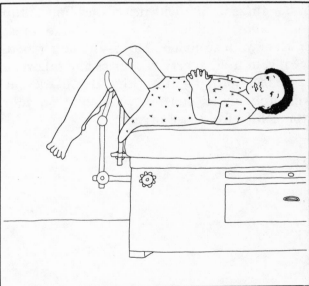

The doctor or health worker will first look at your genitals and see that everything is healthy. Then she will check your internal organs. To do this, she will use a *speculum* (SPECK-you-lum). A speculum is either metal or plastic. It is inserted into your vagina to hold the vaginal walls apart. Then something called a pap smear is taken. A cotton swab is gently touched in your cervical opening to collect some of your cervical tissues. You probably won't feel this at all. These cells are put on a slide and sent to a laboratory. The pap smear is a check to make sure the cells in your cervix are growing normally.

Then the speculum will be removed. The gynecologist will put on a pair of thin rubber gloves. She'll apply a special slippery *gel* (JEL) to her fingers. She will insert one finger into your vagina and with the other hand press down on your stomach. This is the best way to see if your uterus, cervix, ovaries and fallopian tubes feel normal and healthy. If you ask, she will probably let you put your hand on your stomach to feel these organs.

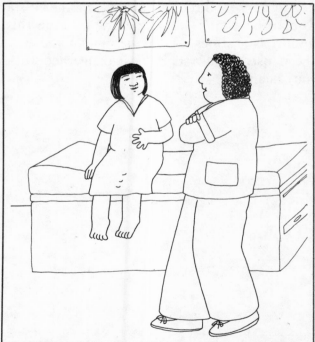

If you have any questions, ask them during your exam. You might even want to make a list to take into the room with you so you don't forget anything. Doctors sometimes don't give much information unless you ask. They've done this many times before and don't realize that you might not know all about it yourself. But remember, it's your body, and you have every right to learn as much as you want about it.

The most important thing to remember about gynecology is to have anything that seems unusual checked out. If you have been feeling anything different around your genitals, like burning or itching or seeing a new kind of discharge (fluid which comes from your vagina), tell your gynecologist. If your breasts hurt or you have any lumps in them, ask your doctor about it. Often when a girl's breasts are growing, there is some tenderness, but a doctor will be able to make sure everything is all right. The more you tell your doctor or health worker, the better and more complete exam she will be able to give you. The better your exam is, the healthier you will be and, after all, that's what we're all aiming for with our pelvic exams.

Conclusion

Well, here we are at the end of this book. We hope you enjoyed looking at it and that it answered many of your questions. There are two important things we'd like you to remember. One is that no two people are ever quite the same.

The other is that we want you to ask questions and get answers to the things about your life that you don't understand. After reading this book, you know more about menstruation than the three of us knew when we were nine or ten years old. We learned a lot about menstruation just writing the book, and when we talked with some of our friends (girls and women both) we found that often they didn't know about some of these things either. We hope that knowing how your body works makes growing up and going through all these changes easier.

Good luck!

JoAnn Gardner-Loulan   **Bonnie Lopez**   **Marcia Quackenbush**

JoAnn Gardner-Loulan is currently in private practice as a psychotherapist in the San Francisco Bay Area. She is a mother, author and lecturer. She authors books, chapters for anthologies and articles on topics of sexuality and self-esteem. Her lecturing has taken her all over the U.S., Canada and parts of Europe. Her mothering has taken her everywhere.

Bonnie Lopez is now working within the telecommunications industry by day and facilitating women's sexuality groups by night. Her son Daniel, 10, and daughter Katy, 7, have read this book many, many times and still have questions!

So, readers, keep the conversations ongoing and open-ended.

Marcia Quackenbush is a licensed Marriage, Family & Child Counselor and sees clients in private practice. She has been active in HIV and AIDS work since 1984, and is an author of several AIDS-related publications, including *Teaching AIDS: A Resource Guide on Acquired Immune Deficiency Syndrome*; *The AIDS Challenge: Prevention Education for Young People*; and *Does AIDS Hurt? Educating Young Children About AIDS*. She is also an illustrator and photographer and plans to continue writing and illustrating books focusing on health issues of importance to children and teenagers.

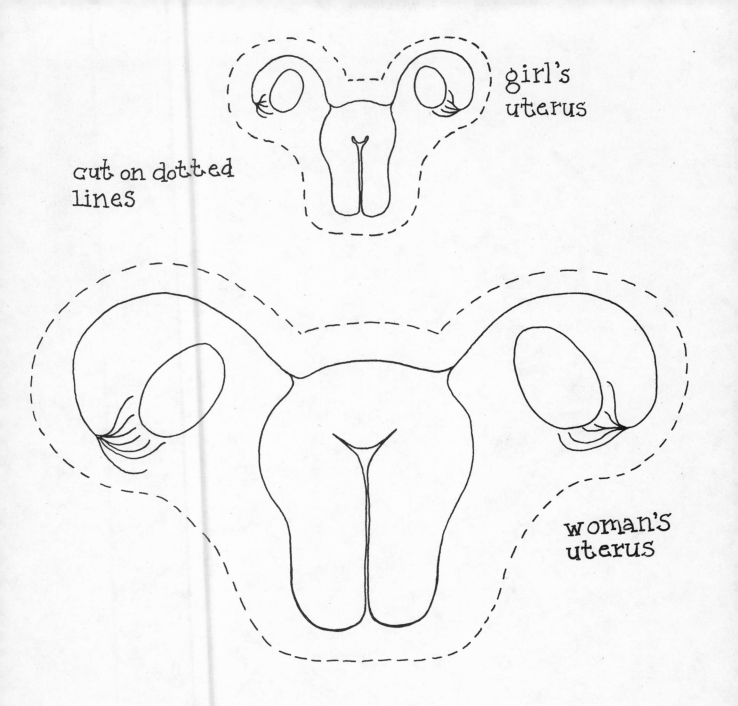

girl's
uterus

cut on dotted
lines

woman's
uterus

PARENTS' GUIDE

Talking About
Menstruation
With Your Children

from **PERIOD.** Updated 1991

VOLCANO
PRESS

iris

It has now been almost fifteen years since the three of us first began working on *Period.* We are all surprised at how quickly the time has passed.

When we wrote *Period.*, we talked for hours with one another about our experiences growing up and asked dozens of friends and acquaintances about their experiences as well. We wrote the book from the perspective of our own memories and those of our friends.

Today our lives have changed. Bonnie has two children, JoAnn has one, and Marcia has three nieces and five nephews. As we watch the children around us grow up, we try to help them understand the world around them and their own always-changing bodies. Now, a new perspective comes to mind: "How can parents and other adults in children's lives best help them understand this process of growing up? How should we tell our daughters, and our sons, about bodily changes and menstruation?"

Once again, we got together and talked about our experiences. We asked our friends how they approached these issues with their children. We have gathered some stories to share and some ideas to pass on to help you talk to your children about these important concerns.

Bonnie's story: *Since they were first born, my children Daniel and Katy have been with me at times in the bathroom. Katy is six now. She has noticed my once-a-month menstrual period and has had countless questions over the years. Her first questions came before she was one year old.*

We have many books around our home which explain how bodies grow and where babies come from. Katy, Daniel and I have spent hours together looking at the books and talking about the pictures.

*A couple of months ago, Katy was with me while I was changing a tampon. "Mom," she said, "exactly why **do** you wear that thing?"*

*I was flabbergasted! Of any child **she** should have known the answer to that question!*

Topics concerning our bodies and their development, pregnancy and conception, menstruation and growing up are a constant source of interest and learning for children. They want to know about the nitty-gritty aspects of bodily development: smells, fluids, "bad words," what a tampon feels like in your vagina, whether menstruation hurts. They giggle or make faces — "Oh, yuck!" — but they love to know the answers.

Children also learn things in stages, sometimes in very small steps. They remember information they use regularly and forget things that don't seem as important. This is why so many parents who feel they have already thoroughly covered certain topics find basic questions coming up over and over again. Talking with our children about "growing up" is something parents can do for their children throughout their lives. It will never be covered in one or two well-timed discussions. This is a matter we can bring into our lives with our children on a regular basis.

Marcia's story: *My mother has always been an easy person to talk to about bodily changes and growing older. As a pre-adolescent, I remember going to her with lots of questions about all the new feelings I was having and couldn't understand. As I got older, we would sometimes talk for hours about the things I was learning at school, my relationships with friends, or how I felt about the world. Every now and then, not often, I would*

3

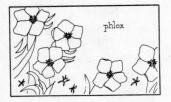
phlox

talk to her about the ways my body was changing and how I was growing up. She was consistently supportive and understanding.

Now, in my mid-thirties, I still have these kinds of discussions with my mother and my father. I talk about the physical changes I experience as I age, and the greater wisdom I am gaining as I grow older. They tell me what aging has been like for them, and help me feel positive about the process. I have talked with my parents about their feelings about death and whether they are afraid of dying. These kinds of talks help me feel I know them better, and they also help me know myself. I am pleased that they have made "talking about growing up" an ongoing part of our relationship.

Children may benefit from hearing about growing up from many different adults. Mothers, fathers, grandparents, aunts and uncles, good family friends — all may have something to contribute to a child's understanding. Each family will be different in how they go about sharing this information.

Aaron's story: I believe that how I feel about my own body is more important than anything I can say to my children about growing up. When they see that I feel good about myself, they learn to feel good about themselves as well. Showing affection is important too, and a lot of fathers don't necessarily hug their children that much.

I have never actually had a direct conversation with my daughter or my son about the technical details of growing up. We have books around that explain these things, and I know my wife has talked to our daughter about menstruation and

our son about wet dreams. She seems to handle these things more comfortably than I do. But I do make sure that such matters have been covered with the children. Then I take part by being available to talk about the emotional details. In our family, this has worked really well.

JoAnn's story: I gave a copy of Period. to my niece Amy when she was six. She was so excited about it, she sat down right then and there to read the book. This was during a big family gathering — Amy's older sisters Lisa and Laura (seven and eight) were there. So were her young cousins Jenny and Adam (five and three). Add in Amy's parents, her grandparents, another aunt and uncle, and you can see we had quite a group.

Well, all of us sat around the living room while Amy read the book out loud. When she came to a word that was hard to pronounce, or a concept that she couldn't understand, she would ask someone else in the room. We had three generations of the family there, all talking openly about menstruation and cramps, vaginas and tampons — it was great!

This wasn't something we had done before. It's not like we were the original liberal family and we always talked about these things. I am sure Amy's grandparents and parents were uncomfortable and a little embarrassed to be talking about matters that felt so private to them. But the children approached it openly with real excitement and that excitement was infectious. We all helped Amy learn about menstruation and growing up, and she helped all of us learn a new way to be together.

Michael's story: *My wife and I divorced when our children were young and now we share custody. Generally, I see my kids one evening a week and on alternate weekends. And, honestly, I'm aware that I get to be the "fun parent," while my ex-wife has to deal with more of the day-to-day issues about chores and discipline and homework.*

One of the men I work with mentioned something the other day about his eleven-year-old beginning to menstruate and I realized that my daughter Christie is nine now. I've sort of assumed all along that her mom would discuss these growing up issues with her. And probably she has. But I don't know for sure, and even if her mom has, I don't really know what she has said to Christie. Like a lot of other divorced couples we try to stay on top of things, but our communication is not always great.

*Well, I thought, why should I deprive my daughter of **my** feelings about growing up? I'd like her to hear about some of my experiences, and I really want to hear about hers. I talked this over with her mom and let her know I was going to have some talks of my own with Christie. Then I bought Christie a copy of* Period. *and we started talking about it. It's hard for me sometimes, but it's really worth it because I have this whole new opportunity to get to know my daughter better.*

Of course, stories like this tend to make it all sound pretty easy. You always hear about everyone's successes. When you think about bringing up these issues with your own children, the situation may seem very different from the experiences here. Raelyn's story might sound more familiar.

Raelyn's story: *My daughter Tiffany is eleven, which is how old I was when I started to menstruate. I know she's had some education about menstruation in school, so it won't come as a total surprise to her, but I feel like I should talk with her about my own experiences too.*

The problem is that we just never did things like this in my family. No one ever talked about menstruation with me, and I was terrified when I started my periods. Knowing my family, I am sure it was the same for my mother and my grandmother.

*I've read suggestions in magazine articles — "Be sure to have some books about growing up in your library at home," they tell you. Big help! We don't **have** a library at home. I don't read much and neither do my kids, and I really don't have the money to spend on books like that. They're expensive.*

"Just start in talking with your child, and admit your discomfort or embarrassment," they say. Great idea. I tried this once with Tiffany — I gave her a book to read and told her I wanted to talk about it with her when she was done. She never read the book. Then I said one day, "I'm really nervous about this, but I feel because I'm your mother I should talk to you about growing up." She tried to leave the room.

"Come back here, young lady!" I scolded, thinking all along this isn't how it was supposed to be going.

"I just wonder if you have any questions about these things — menstruation, your body's changes . . . you know."

"Mom! Please!" she wailed. And she

hyacinth

wouldn't say another word. I finally had to let her go, and she went and watched TV for the rest of the night.

*I just don't see how I can do this with **my** kid.*

In the beginning of *Period.*, we talk about how magazines and movies make everyone look beautiful and perfect, as if they have no problems at all. Parent guides sometimes do the same thing, and a parent can easily feel like something is wrong if his or her children won't talk about growing up even when the suggestions in the books and magazine articles are followed. We know how hard these things can be, and we've made lots of mistakes with our own children. But one of the things we've also found is if you keep trying and you don't have unrealistic expectations of yourself or your children, you can have some rewarding experiences together.

What can you expect from your children? First, you might think about how your children respond when you talk to them about things other than growing up. Do you have long conversations with them about how to vacuum or do the dishes? About the price of oranges at the grocery this week? About how to make and keep friends? How to do their homework efficiently?

Most children are fairly selective about what they say to their parents. Some topics are easier to discuss than others. Many children who are eight or ten or twelve hardly talk to their parents about anything at all. Children these ages do spend a lot of time talking to their peers.

We may assume because they don't talk back to us, they aren't listening to what we have to say. This is not necessarily true. Most children are good listeners,

and sometimes they're even "sly" listeners — overhearing things we would rather they not hear at all! But they also tend to have a short attention span, and they may be uncomfortable about how to respond to the things you say.

And what can you expect from yourself? Expect to feel awkward, expect to make mistakes, and expect to feel frustrated. When your "growing up talk" with your child doesn't flow the nice easy way it did on the television sitcom last week, don't blame yourself. And most importantly, expect that this will get easier and better with practice.

You can choose moments to talk to your child when you are in your car or on the bus, while you're preparing dinner together, or during a commercial while you're watching television. You might just say something about growing up. Start with a personal comment. "You're ten years old now. You know, when I was ten I started menstruating. I don't think we've ever even talked together about periods." Don't expect a conversation, and don't put your child on the spot with questions. Make a few comments, and then move on to another topic.

And once you've done that, what next? You'll want some fresh material for the next short discussion. There are lots of different possibilities:

- If you're a woman, talk about your own experiences beginning to menstruate — when you started, how it felt, how your family responded, the sorts of things your friends said.

- If you're a man, talk about when you first learned about menstruation and what you and other boys your age thought and felt about it.

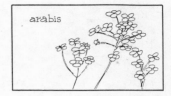
arabis

- Respond to advertisements about tampons, menstrual pads, feminine hygiene sprays, douches.

- Talk about the things your mother and father said, or didn't say, to you about growing up.

- Describe the movies about menstruation you saw in school.

- Glance through books or pamphlets about menstruation, or the inserts in tampon packages, and discuss them with your child.

- Talk about the myths you heard about menstruation while you were growing up. Ask your child if she has ever heard such things, and correct the myths:
    "You can't take baths during your period."
    "You can't get pregnant while you're menstruating."
    "You shouldn't go swimming during your period."
    "Don't do any vigorous exercise."
    "Cramps are imaginary."
    "Don't let yourself get chilled during your period or you will get a cold."
    "Women are always irritable or nervous during their periods."

- Look at the chapter in this book called, "Why Do I Feel This Way?" Take each feeling, one at a time, and use it as a topic for a talk with your child.

- Read other chapters in the book and bring up important points from the chapter with your child.

- Bring up other memories of your childhood and adolescence having to do with growing up generally. This helps set the context for continuing discussions of this nature.

There are many more possibilities, but these ideas can get you going. If it still seems difficult, you might make a commitment to bring up menstruation or growing up with your child at least once a week for the next month.

These talks can be a fine opportunity to share some of your own vulnerabilities with your child. You can talk about the difficulties you faced as a young person, about times you were afraid of or confused by your body's changes. You can let your child see that the two of you have had some similar experiences. By letting our children see that we have gone through these kinds of events, that we have survived and even learned from them, we are helping them learn that this is a normal process and that they will survive it too.

Once your child is used to you bringing these topics up in little bits, you can move to lengthier discussions. Over time, your child may feel more comfortable asking you questions and really discussing these things. But don't worry too much if she doesn't. She is listening to you, and your continued efforts demonstrate to her that these are important issues to you and that you care very deeply for her.

You might try some other activities as well. You could ask your daughter to plan a special celebration with you that you'll carry out when she starts her first

tiger lily

period. Would she like a family dinner, a slumber party with her girlfriends, a dinner at a restaurant with you, tickets to a play?

You could write your daughter a letter, including some of your own memories of growing up and your feelings about how she is growing up. This gives her a keepsake — something she can read in private, look over again in the future, save with her special things if she wants.

You could take a trip to a local hospital and look at the newborn babies with her. For girls who have not been around tiny babies, this can be very exciting. It gives you another opportunity to talk about what she was like when she was an infant, the ways she has changed since then, and how she will continue to change as she matures.

A note about boys: *Period.* was written specifically for pre-menstrual girls, but we know parents who have bought the book for their young sons. Boys need to know about growing up too. Often, menstruation gets left out of their education and becomes a mysterious and mystifying event. If you have sons, be sure to tell them about how they will change as they grow up, and talk to them about the changes girls also go through.

A few final suggestions: When you talk with your children, try to share with them your own sense of wonder at the ways they have grown and changed. Sit down with them and look over their baby pictures. Let them be inspired by your own pride in them, so they can feel good about themselves and the ways they are growing.

As you continue to talk about these things, you will find it getting easier to do. When you feel unsure, or frustrated, or intimidated, think about how you would act if you knew exactly what you were doing and felt totally confident. Then act as if this were actually the case. Acting "as if" is a great technique to get us past our stumbling blocks, and it really works.

Involve other parents in your community in efforts to educate children about growing up. Sometimes, community organizations will plan parent-child workshops about growing up, and these can be very successful. You can check with your church, a school nurse, local Planned Parenthood chapters, or community groups such as the Girls' Club, Girl Scouts, YWCA, etc.

We may have to put a fair amount of effort into these ongoing communications with our children. Sometimes we aren't sure what to say or do, and sometimes we don't feel all that great about the changes our own bodies are going through. It takes work on our part to give our children a legacy of pride and wonder in the workings of their bodies and all they can do.

What a truly precious gift we offer them when we succeed!

The Parents' Guide is a pull-out supplement from **PERIOD.**, Updated 1991, by JoAnn Gardner-Loulan, Bonnie Lopez and Marcia Quackenbush.
It can be ordered directly from the publisher, or from your local bookstore.
$9.95 paperback   ISBN 0-912078-88-X
Please include $3.00 postage and handling for the first book ordered, and $.75 for each additional book.
California residents: Please add 6% sales tax.
Schools, agencies and organizations please contact Volcano Press directly for quantity discounts.

Volcano Press
P.O. Box 270
Volcano CA 95689
(209) 296-3445   FAX: (209) 296-4515